THE OFFICIAL
MANCHESTER UNITED®
Times
Tables
Book

PAUL BROADBENT

Letts

KICK-OFF

The Manchester United books are a fun way to learn and practise your Maths skills. Each book contains: **11 Big Matches, a flick-a-book player, find the cup, a poster and a board game!**

The Big Matches

Learn a new skill

Practise the skill

Flick the pages and make the player move

Play the match
- Test your skills (answers on 26–27)

- Colour in the Testometer to mark your score

See if you can find the cup hidden in each unit!

Enjoy the pull-out game and poster in the middle of the book!

The Game

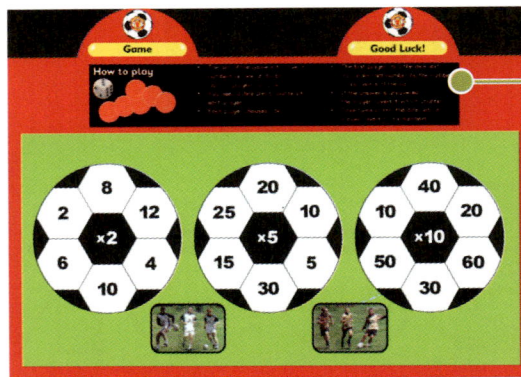

What you need and how to play

The Poster

Collect all the books in the series and the six individual posters make one big poster!

Contents

TRAINING

Grouping in twos and threes

Grouping objects is a good way of counting.

The socks are in groups of **2**

There are **4** groups of **2**

This makes **8** socks altogether.

Practise your skills

A **Ring these players in groups of two. Count the groups.**

1

☐ twos
☐ players

2

☐ twos
☐ players

3

☐ twos
☐ players

B **Draw footballs in each of these goals. Group them in threes.**

6 footballs → ☐2☐ threes

1

9 footballs →

☐ threes

2

15 footballs →

☐ threes

3

12 footballs →

☐ threes

Big Match 1

Colour in your score on the shirts!

Ring these in groups of two. Count the groups.

1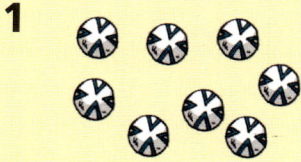
2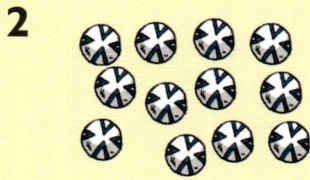
3

8 footballs → ☐ twos   12 footballs → ☐ twos   10 footballs → ☐ twos

4
5

14 footballs → ☐ twos   6 footballs → ☐ twos

Ring these in groups of three. Count the groups.

6
7
8

9 footballs → ☐ threes   6 footballs → ☐ threes   12 footballs → ☐ threes

9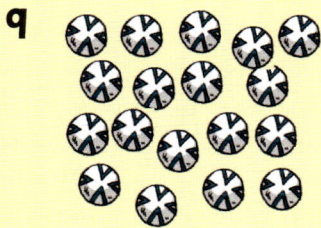
10

18 footballs → ☐ threes   15 footballs → ☐ threes

10 9 8 7 6 5 4 3 2 1

vodafone

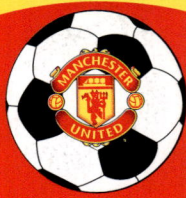

Repeated addition

3 + 3 + 3 + 3

4 lots of 3 are **12**

Practise your skills

A   Write how many.

1

☐ fingers on 2 gloves

2

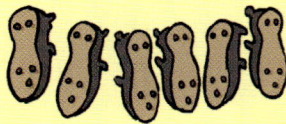

☐ studs on 6 boots

3

☐ arms on 4 shirts

0 1 2 3 4 5 6 7 8 9 10 11 12 13 14 15 16 17 18 19 20

B   Use the number line to help you with these sums.

1   3 jumps of 5 are ☐

2   4 jumps of 3 are ☐

3   5 jumps of 2 are ☐

4   4 jumps of 4 are ☐

Colour in your score on the exercising players!

Write the answers.

1 5 lots of 2 → ☐

2 4 lots of 3 → ☐

3 2 lots of 4 → ☐

4 3 lots of 5 → ☐

5 6 lots of 2 → ☐

6 4 lots of 4 → ☐

7 5 lots of 3 → ☐

8 2 lots of 10 → ☐

9 3 lots of 4 → ☐

10 4 lots of 5 → ☐

When Phil and Gary Neville both played for England in 1996 it was the first time a national team had brothers in it since the Charlton brothers in the 1960s.

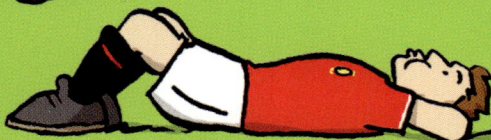

10
9
8
7
6
5
4
3
2
1

Counting in twos and threes

This ball is headed in jumps of **two**.

This ball is headed in **threes**.

Practise your skills

A **Start at 0. Colour the pattern of twos.**

0 1 2 3 4 5 6 7 8 9 10 11 12 13 14 15 16 17 18 19 20

B **Start at 0. Colour the pattern of threes.**

0 1 2 3 4 5 6 7 8 9 10 11 12 13 14 15 16 17 18 19 20

C **Write the missing numbers.**

0 2 ☐ ☐ 8 10 ☐ ☐ ☐ ☐

0 3 6 ☐ ☐ ☐ 18 ☐ ☐ ☐

Colour in your score on the scarf!

Write the next number in each pattern.

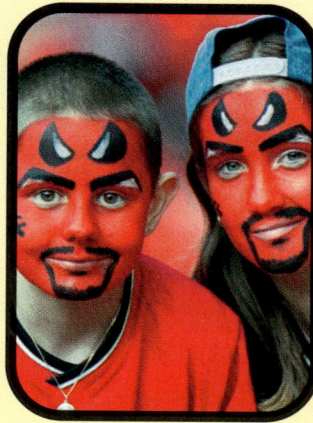

1 2 4 6 8 10 ___

2 8 10 12 14 ___

3 3 6 9 ___

4 15 18 21 24 ___

5 16 18 ___

Write the missing numbers.

6 8 10 ___ 14 16 ___

7 6 ___ ___ 15 18 21

8 ___ 4 6 ___ 10 12

9 9 12 15 ___ 21 ___

10 ___ 12 14 16 ___ 20

10
9
8
7
6
5
4
3
2
1

9

Two times table

Remember: 3 × 2 gives the same answer as 2 × 3

3 + 3 = 6
2 lots of 3 = 6
2 × 3 = 6

2 + 2 + 2 = 6
3 lots of 2 = 6
3 × 2 = 6

Practise your skills

Answer these.

1 4 × 2 = ☐
   2 × 4 = ☐

2 5 × 2 = ☐
   2 × 5 = ☐

3 8 × 2 = ☐
   2 × 8 = ☐

4 6 × 2 = ☐
   2 × 6 = ☐

5 7 × 2 = ☐
   2 × 7 = ☐

Big Match 4

Answer these.

1 6 × 2 = ☐

2 4 × 2 = ☐

3 3 × 2 = ☐

4 5 × 2 = ☐

5 1 × 2 = ☐

6 9 × 2 = ☐

7 7 × 2 = ☐

8 2 × 2 = ☐

9 10 × 2 = ☐

10 8 × 2 = ☐

Colour in your score on the kit!

10
9
8
7
6
5
4
3
2
1

TRAINING

Number patterns

Use this grid to help spot number patterns.

1	2	3	4	5	6	7	8	9	10
11	12	13	14	15	16	17	18	19	20
21	22	23	24	25	26	27	28	29	30
31	32	33	34	35	36	37	38	39	40
41	42	43	44	45	46	47	48	49	50

Practise your skills

A Count in twos

1 6 – 8 – ◯ – ◯ – ◯

2 20 – 18 – ◯ – ◯ – ◯

B Count in threes

1 6 – 9 – ◯ – ◯ – ◯

2 27 – 24 – ◯ – ◯ – ◯

C Count in fours

1 12 – 16 – ◯ – ◯ – ◯

2 40 – 36 – ◯ – ◯ – ◯

D Count in fives

1 5 – 10 – ◯ – ◯ – ◯

2 45 – 40 – ◯ – ◯ – ◯

E Colour all the even numbers. Who wears this number for Manchester United?

_ _ _ _ _ _ _ _ _

3	7	6	14	2	15	4	13	14	5	1	17	6	9	3
9	11	8	7	3	11	2	19	7	2	7	18	7	15	5
5	7	16	12	10	19	16	11	3	7	10	3	1	17	19
15	3	7	15	4	13	8	17	5	4	15	2	9	13	1
19	17	14	18	6	5	10	3	8	7	17	11	16	5	13

Big Match 5

Write the missing number in each pattern.

Colour in your score on the coaches!

1. 8   12   ⬜   20   24
2. 9   12   15   ⬜   21
3. 10   12   ⬜   16   18
4. 10   ⬜   20   25   30
5. 30   40   ⬜   60   70
6. 30   27   ⬜   21   18
7. 60   ⬜   40   30   20
8. 45   40   35   ⬜   25
9. 20   18   16   14   ⬜
10. 32   ⬜   24   20   16

10 9 8 7 6 5 4 3 2 1

MANCHESTER UTD FC

MANCHESTER UTD FC

13

TRAINING

Grouping in fours and fives

When you group in fours and fives, check that each group has the right number in it.

The players are in groups of **4**.

There are **3** groups of **4**.

This makes **12** players altogether.

Practise your skills

A Ring these in groups of four. Count the groups.

1

2

3

| | fours |
| | footballs |

| | fours |
| | footballs |

| | fours |
| | footballs |

B Ring these in groups of five. Count the groups.

1

2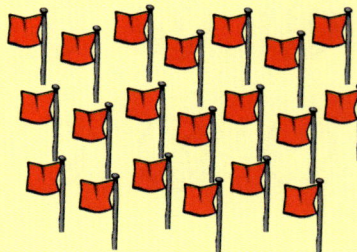

3

| | fives |
| | flags |

| | fives |
| | flags |

| | fives |
| | flags |

Good Luck!

...s to cover 6
...e balls.
...ay
...counters for

...ball.

- The first player rolls the dice and multiplies that number by the number in the centre of the ball.
- If the answer is uncovered, the player covers it with a counter.
- Take turns to roll the dice until a player covers all six numbers.

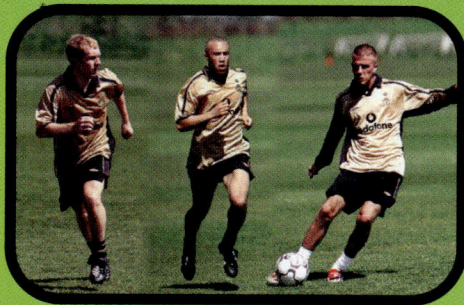

10

5

40   10   20

x10

50   60

30

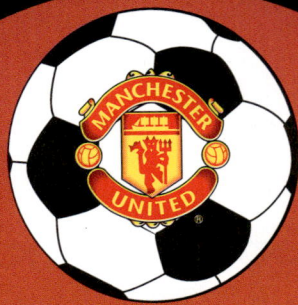

Game

How to play

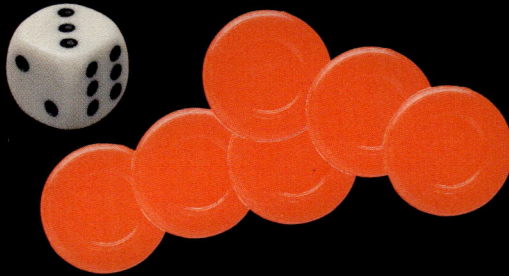

- The aim of the ga[me]
  numbers on one o[f]
  Up to 3 players c[an]
- You need a dice a[nd]
  each player.
- Each player choos[es]

Big Match 6

Answer these questions.

1 6 groups of 4 → ☐

2 3 groups of 4 → ☐

3 5 groups of 4 → ☐

4 8 groups of 4 → ☐

5 10 groups of 4 → ☐

6 3 groups of 5 → ☐

7 5 groups of 5 → ☐

8 8 groups of 5 → ☐

9 4 groups of 5 → ☐

10 6 groups of 5 → ☐

Colour in your score on the winning players!

At only 12 years old David Beckham won a Bobby Charlton Soccer Skills award which was presented at Old Trafford.

15

Counting in fives and tens

Look at the pattern of fives and tens.

Practise your skills

A Colour the numbers in the 5 times table **red**.

B Draw a circle around the numbers in the 10 times table.

1	2	3	4	5	6	7	8	9	10
11	12	13	14	15	16	17	18	19	20
21	22	23	24	25	26	27	28	29	30
31	32	33	34	35	36	37	38	39	40
41	42	43	44	45	46	47	48	49	50
51	52	53	54	55	56	57	58	59	60
61	62	63	64	65	66	67	68	69	70
71	72	73	74	75	76	77	78	79	80
81	82	83	84	85	86	87	88	89	90
91	92	93	94	95	96	97	98	99	100

C Write the missing numbers.

1 | 5 | 10 | | 20 | | 30 | | | 45 | |

2 | 10 | | 30 | | | 60 | 70 | | | |

16

Big Match 7

Colour in your score on the cones and striker!

Write the missing numbers.

1 | 5 | 10 | | 20 | 25 | |

2 | 30 | | | 60 | 70 | 80 |

3 | 15 | | 25 | | 35 | 40 |

4 | 80 | | 60 | 50 | | 30 |

5 | | 30 | 25 | 20 | | 10 |

Write the answers.

6 7 tens are [ ]

7 6 fives are [ ]

8 3 tens are [ ]

9 9 fives are [ ]

10 8 tens are [ ]

Manchester United FC prefer to play on wet grass, this makes the pitch slicker and faster which suits their style of play.

Five and ten times table

Try to learn your 5 and 10 times tables. The patterns are easy to remember.

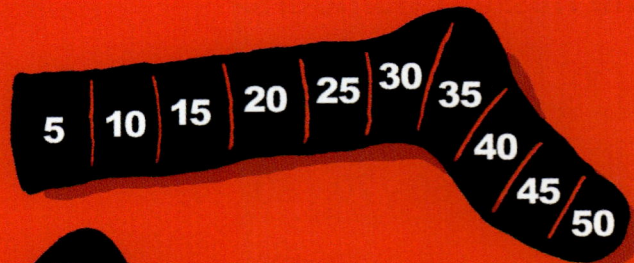

| 5 | 10 | 15 | 20 | 25 | 30 | 35 |
| | | | | | 40 | 45 | 50 |

| 10 |
| 20 |
| 30 | 40 | 50 | 60 | 70 | 80 | 90 | 100 |

Practise your skills

A This attacker can only run through numbers in the 5 times table. Colour them **red**.

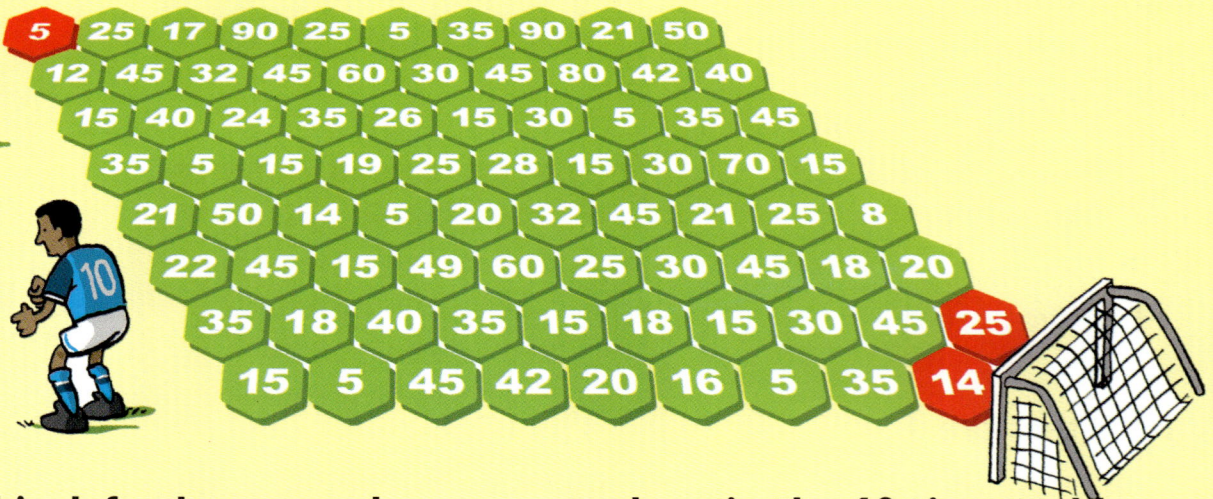

5	25	17	90	25	5	35	90	21	50
12	45	32	45	60	30	45	80	42	40
15	40	24	35	26	15	30	5	35	45
35	5	15	19	25	28	15	30	70	15
21	50	14	5	20	32	45	21	25	8
22	45	15	49	60	25	30	45	18	20
35	18	40	35	15	18	15	30	45	25
15	5	45	42	20	16	5	35	14

B This defender can only go on numbers in the 10 times table. Draw a cross on them.

C Can the attacker score a goal? _____
Draw a line to show the route.

Big Match 8

Colour in your score on the MUFC items!

Answer these sums.

1 6 × 5 = ☐

2 4 × 10 = ☐

3 3 × 5 = ☐

4 7 × 10 = ☐

5 9 × 5 = ☐

6 8 × 10 = ☐

7 5 × 5 = ☐

8 3 × 10 = ☐

9 8 × 5 = ☐

10 9 × 10 = ☐

The Manchester United Soccer School travels the country to coach children in football skills.

19

Times tables

Try to learn your times tables.
Answer them as quickly as you can.

$$3 \times 2 = 6$$

Practise your skills

A Match the boots to a football.

2 × 5   7 × 5   3 × 4

6 × 10   10   40   3 × 7

5 × 6   15   24   4 × 10

16   30

21

8 × 2   12   60   35   3 × 5

B Write a multiplication
fact for the extra football. _____

Answer these as quickly as you can.

1 3×4 =

2 5×5 =

3 2×7 =

4 3×2 =

5 8×5 =

6 9×10 =

7 6×2 =

8 7×5 =

9 6×3 =

10 10×4 =

Colour in your score on the queuing supporters!

Inside Old Trafford there is the official Manchester United FC museum which is packed full of everything you ever wanted to know about the club.

Multiplication facts

When you see missing numbers, use the other numbers to help work it out.

$3 \times ? = 15$ How many 3s make 15?

$$3 \times 5 = 15$$

Practise your skills

A Write the missing numbers.

1

$4 \times \square = 20$

$\square \times 2 = 20$

$\square \times 5 = 20$

$10 \times \square = 20$

2

$\square \times 10 = 30$

$3 \times \square = 30$

$5 \times \square = 30$

3

$2 \times \square = 16$

$\square \times 4 = 16$

$\square \times 8 = 16$

B Write your own facts.

$\square \times \square = 18$

$\square \times \square = 18$

$\square \times \square = 18$

Colour in your score on the film of the match!

Write the missing numbers.

1 $3 \times \bigcirc = 12$

2 $5 \times \bigcirc = 25$

3 $\bigcirc \times 2 = 16$

4 $4 \times \bigcirc = 20$

5 $\bigcirc \times 10 = 70$

6 $\bigcirc \times 3 = 18$

7 $4 \times \bigcirc = 16$

8 $\bigcirc \times 2 = 8$

9 $6 \times \bigcirc = 30$

10 $5 \times \bigcirc = 50$

Manchester United FC began its life in 1878 as Newton Heath LYR. Its players were all workers from the local railway.

Multiplying and dividing

There is a close link between multiplication and division.

$2 \times 3 = 6$

$6 \div 2 = 3$

6 grouped into 2s is **3**

$\div$ is the sign for 'divided by'

Practise your skills

A   Use the code wheel to find some Manchester United Stars.

1 $12 \div 2 = \boxed{6}$ $8 \div 2 = \square$ $6 \div 2 = \square$ $16 \div 2 = \square$ $18 \div 2 = \square$

$\underline{B}$ $\underline{}$ $\underline{}$ $\underline{}$ $\underline{}$ Z

2 $18 \div 3 = \square$ $20 \div 2 = \square$ $16 \div 2 = \square$ $80 \div 10 = \square$

$\underline{}$ $\underline{}$ $\underline{}$ $\underline{}$

3 $25 \div 5 = \square$ $40 \div 5 = \square$ $20 \div 5 = \square$ $5 \div 5 = \square$

$\underline{}$ $\underline{}$ $\underline{}$ $\underline{}$

4 $14 \div 2 = \square$ $20 \div 10 = \square$ $35 \div 5 = \square$ $21 \div 3 = \square$ $15 \div 3 = \square$

$\underline{}$ $\underline{}$ $\underline{}$ $\underline{}$ $\underline{}$

Big Match 11

Write the missing numbers.

Colour in your score on the weights!

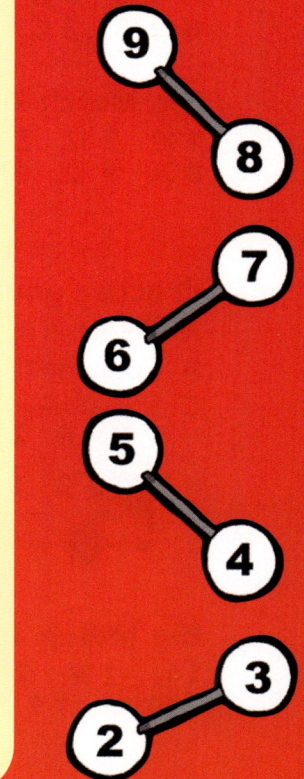

1 $2 \times \boxed{} = 8$ $\qquad$ $8 \div 2 = \boxed{}$

2 $3 \times \boxed{} = 12$ $\qquad$ $12 \div 3 = \boxed{}$

3 $5 \times \boxed{} = 25$ $\qquad$ $25 \div 5 = \boxed{}$

4 $2 \times \boxed{} = 14$ $\qquad$ $14 \div 2 = \boxed{}$

5 $3 \times \boxed{} = 15$ $\qquad$ $15 \div 3 = \boxed{}$

6 $\boxed{} \times 3 = 9$ $\qquad$ $9 \div 3 = \boxed{}$

7 $\boxed{} \times 5 = 20$ $\qquad$ $20 \div 5 = \boxed{}$

8 $\boxed{} \times 2 = 16$ $\qquad$ $16 \div 2 = \boxed{}$

9 $\boxed{} \times 5 = 15$ $\qquad$ $15 \div 5 = \boxed{}$

10 $\boxed{} \times 10 = 40$ $\qquad$ $40 \div 10 = \boxed{}$

There are over 200 official Manchester United FC supporters' clubs found all over the world.

10 9 8 7 6 5 4 3 2 1

Answers

Grouping in twos and threes 4–5
Practise your skills

A Check groups are circled correctly.
 1 3 twos, 6 players
 2 5 twos, 10 players
 3 6 twos, 12 players
B Check correct amount of balls are drawn.
 1 3 threes
 2 5 threes
 3 4 threes

Big Match 1
Check groups are circled correctly.
 1 4 **2** 6 **3** 5 **4** 7 **5** 3
 6 3 **7** 2 **8** 4 **9** 6 **10** 5

Repeated addition 6–7
Practise your skills

A 1 10 **2** 30 **3** 8
B 1 15 **2** 12 **3** 10 **4** 16

Big Match 2
 1 10 **2** 12 **3** 8 **4** 15 **5** 12 **6** 16 **7** 15
 8 20 **9** 12 **10** 20

Counting in twos and threes.......8–9
Practise your skills

A Colour in 0, 2, 4, 6, 8, 10, 12, 14, 16, 18, 20.
B Colour in 0, 3, 6, 9, 12, 15, 18.
C

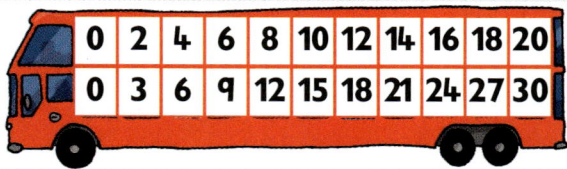

0	2	4	6	8	10	12	14	16	18	20
0	3	6	9	12	15	18	21	24	27	30

Big Match 3
 1 12 **2** 16 **3** 12 **4** 27 **5** 20
 6 12, 18 **7** 9, 12 **8** 2, 8 **9** 18, 24 **10** 10, 18

Two times table 10–11
Practise your skills

 1 8, 8 **2** 10, 10 **3** 16, 16 **4** 12, 12 **5** 14, 14

Big Match 4
 1 12 **2** 8 **3** 6 **4** 10 **5** 2 **6** 18 **7** 14
 8 4 **9** 20 **10** 16

Number patterns............................12
Practise your skills

A 1 10, 12, 14 **2** 16, 14, 12
B 1 12, 15, 18 **2** 21, 18, 15
C 1 20, 24, 28 **2** 32, 28, 24
D 1 15, 20, 25 **2** 35, 30, 25
E Japp Stam

Big Match 5
 1 16 **2** 18 **3** 14 **4** 15 **5** 50 **6** 24 **7** 50
 8 30 **9** 12 **10** 28

Grouping in fours and fives 14–15
Practise your skills

A Check groups are circled correctly.
 1 2 fours, 8 footballs
 2 4 fours, 16 footballs
 3 5 fours, 20 footballs
B Check groups are circled correctly.
 1 2 fives, 10 flags
 2 4 fives, 20 flags
 3 3 fives, 15 flags

Big Match 6
 1 24 **2** 12 **3** 20 **4** 32 **5** 40 **6** 15 **7** 25
 8 40 **9** 20 **10** 30

Answers

Counting in fives and tens 16–17
Practise your skills

A Colour red 5, 15,25, 35, 45, 55, 65, 75, 85, 95.

B Circle 10, 20, 30, 40, 50, 60, 70, 80, 90, 100.

C 1 15, 25, 35, 40, 50
   2 20, 40, 50, 80, 90, 100

Big Match 7
1 15, 30   **2** 40, 50   **3** 20, 30   **4** 70, 40
5 35, 15   **6** 70   **7** 30   **8** 30   **9** 45   **10** 80

Five and ten times table 18–19
Practise your skills

A Colour red the route to the goal 5, 25, 45, 15, 35, 5, 15, 35, 45, 25, 5, 35, 45, 15, 25, 5, 15, 45, 35, 15, 5, 45, 35, 15, 25, 45, 15, 5, 35, 45, 15, 25, 45, 15, 5, 35, 45.
These numbers are also in the 5 times table: 90, 90, 50, 60, 30, 80, 40, 40, 30, 30, 70, 50, 20, 60, 30, 20, 40, 30, 20

B Draw a cross on 90, 90, 50, 60, 30, 80, 40, 40, 30, 30, 70, 50, 20, 60, 30, 20, 40, 30, 20.

C Yes. Check line is drawn correctly.

Big Match 8
1 30   **2** 40   **3** 15   **4** 70   **5** 45   **6** 80   **7** 25
8 30   **9** 40   **10** 90

Times tables 20–21
Practise your skills

A $7 \times 5 = 35$, $3 \times 4 = 12$, $3 \times 7 = 21$
   $4 \times 10 = 40$, $3 \times 5 = 15$, $8 \times 2 = 16$
   $5 \times 6 = 30$, $6 \times 10 = 60$

B 6×4 or $3 \times 8 = 24$ or 4×6 and 8×3

Big Match 9
1 12   **2** 25   **3** 14   **4** 6   **5** 40   **6** 90   **7** 12
8 35   **9** 18   **10** 40

Multiplication facts...................22–23
Practise your skills

A 1 5, 10, 4, 2
   2 3, 10, 6
   3 8, 4, 2

B Answers may vary, check answers.
18×1 1×18
2×9 9×2
6×3 3×6

Big Match 10
1 4   **2** 5   **3** 8   **4** 5   **5** 7   **6** 6   **7** 4   **8** 4
9 5   **10** 10

Multiplying and dividing 24–25
Practise your skills

A 1 4 = A,   3 = R,   8 = T,   9 = E
   2 6 = B,   10 = U,   8 = T,   8 = T
   3 5 = S,   8 = T,   4 = A,   1 = M
   4 7 = G,   2 = I,   7 = G,   7 = G,   5 = S

Big Match 11
1 4, 4   **2** 4, 4   **3** 5, 5   **4** 7, 7   **5** 5, 5
6 3, 3   **7** 4, 4   **8** 8, 8   **9** 3, 3   **10** 4, 4

Collect the set

Collect all 6 books and be an English and Maths champion.

Manchester United English

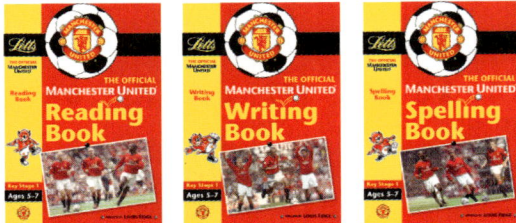

Louis Fidge

Manchester United Maths

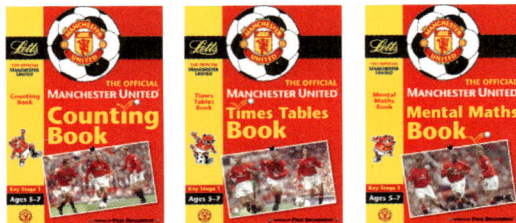

Paul Broadbent

For all the latest news, views and information on

MANCHESTER UNITED®

visit the official Manchester United website:

WWW.MANUTD.COM

Manchester United Plc, Sir Matt Busby Way, Old Trafford, Manchester M16 0RA

Letts Educational, The Chiswick Centre, 414 Chiswick High Road, London W4 5TF
Tel: 020 8996 3333 Fax: 020 8742 8390 E-mail: mail@lettsed.co.uk
Website: www.letts-education.com

Every effort has been made to trace copyright holders and obtain their permission for the use of copyright material. The authors and publishers will gladly receive information enabling them to rectify any error or omission in subsequent editions.

All facts are correct at time of going to press.

Published 2001
Text © Letts Educational Ltd. Published under license from Manchester United Football Club, Video Collection International Limited and Carlton Books Limited. All Trade Marks related to Manchester United Football Club are used with the permission of Manchester United Football Club, Video Collection International Limited and Carlton Books Limited.
Author: Paul Broadbent
Editorial and Design: Moondisks Ltd, Cambridge
Illustrations: Joel Morris
Our thanks to Mark Wylie (MUFC museum curator) and John Peters (MUFC official photographer) for supplying material and their cooperation in the production of these books.

All rights reserved. No part of this publication may be reproduced, stored in a retrieval system, or transmitted, in any form or by any means, electronic, mechanical, photocopying, recording or otherwise, without the prior permission of Letts Educational.

British Library Cataloguing in Publication Data
A CIP record for this book is available from the British Library.

ISBN 1-85805-972-0

Printed in Italy.

Letts Educational Limited is a member of Granada Learning Limited, part of the Granada Media Group.